Essential Considerations for First-Time *Car Buyers*

Money Matters

Essential Considerations for First-Time *Car Buyers*

Money Matters

GAURAV MADHYANI

Worldwide Published by

Pendown Press

PREMIUM BUSINESS PUBLISHER

PENDOWN PRESS LLP
An ISO 9001 & ISO 14001 Certified Co.,
Regd. Office: 3767A, Kanhaiya Nagar,
Tri Nagar, Delhi-110035
Ph.: 8130886000, 9650072927
E-mail: info@pendownpress.com
Branch Office: 1A/2A, 20, Hari Sadan, Ansari Road,
Daryaganj, New Delhi-110002
Ph.: 011-45794768
Website: PendownPress.com

Edition: 2025
Price: ₹ 259
ISBN: 978-93-6338-125-4

Layout and Cover Designed by Pendown Graphics Team
Printed and Bound in India by Thomson Press India Ltd.

CONTENTS

ACKNOWLEDGEMENTS

Writing this book has been a journey filled with gratitude, and I would like to take a moment to acknowledge those who have played a significant role in my life and career.

First and foremost, I want to express my heartfelt gratitude to my uncle, Mr. Kalash Madhyani ji, my business partner since 2014. From the very beginning, we have worked side by side, building a business dedicated to helping people find the right car. His guidance, wisdom, and unwavering support have been instrumental in shaping my career.

A special thank you to my mother, who has always been my pillar. Her resilience and unconditional support have given me the courage to pursue my dreams.

To my loving wife, Kritika, who has been my biggest supporter since our marriage in 2017—your belief in me has been a driving force behind my success. And to my wonderful daughter, Saanvi, whose laughter and presence make every challenge worthwhile, you inspire me every day.

I am also deeply grateful to my incredible team, whose insights from customers have been invaluable in shaping this book. Their dedication and commitment to understanding customer needs have made this journey even more rewarding.

Lastly, to the readers—this book is for you. My goal has always been to make car buying an informed and stress-free experience for the middle-class person, and I intend for this book to serve as a helpful guide in your journey.

With gratitude,

Gaurav Madhyani

Chapter 1

"BABUJI DHEERE CHALNA, CAR ME ZARA SAMBHALNA"

THE JOY & CHALLENGES OF BUYING YOUR FIRST CAR

Apni Toh Gaadi Patri Par - Life Is Sorted

Your first car is a milestone that is hard to forget!

The anticipation of purchasing your first car is filled with excitement and dreams of freedom. Whether for yourself or the family, it's a rite of passage, a milestone that declares to the world and your inner self that you have arrived.

It marks newfound independence & mobility and is an indicator of good financial health.

The thought of cruising down open roads on solo drives, the wind in your hair, with a sense of exhilaration that only comes from having your own vehicle fills you up with joy.

Or it could be the thought of driving your family around in comfort without the hassles of public transport or plans being ruined by the weather that fills you with joy and makes you feel like a great provider.

It could even be the thought of exciting road trips with friends & family that is your motivation to buy your first car.

Irrespective of your motive, buying & using your first car should be a safe, joyful, and value-for-money experience.

Channn Se Jo Toote koi Sapna - A Journey of Shattered Dreams

However, what begins as a journey toward joy can quickly turn into a nightmare. The process of buying a car for the first time can become overwhelming with unexpected challenges and pitfalls.

I have met many first-time buyers who feel disappointed after buying a car. I have always wondered why anyone would be unhappy after buying a new car. I mean, it's a dream come true; ideally, everyone should be happy.

But in reality, when I went deep into understanding the reason behind this, I came to realize that people feel let down by their first car because they are unaware of the facts and knowledge needed to make the right decision.

As a result, later, they feel unhappy that their car is not equipped with features that they required or are not suited to their needs or that they could have bought a better one at the same price.

From navigating complex financing options to decoding unfamiliar technical specs & jargon, the experience can be stressful, leaving you feeling frustrated and disillusioned.

Choosing the right car on gleaming showroom floors and glossy brochures can be a big task. The reality of car buying sets in. Hidden fees, pushy sales tactics, and deceptive advertising can all lead to you ending up with your first car not being your right choice.

What was supposed to be a memorable moment becomes a source of stress and anxiety as you grapple with inflated prices and unmet expectations.

Instead of celebrating a milestone, as you begin using your first car, you find yourself wishing for a simpler, more transparent car-buying experience.

Buying a car for the first time can be even more overwhelming in tier-two cities in India, where the automotive market differs slightly from larger urban centers.

Chapter 2

HOW & WHY THIS BOOK?

The introduction to the book highlights the challenges of first-time car buying, and this might have dampened your enthusiasm a bit. But hey, this book is not meant to put down your joy and excitement for buying your first car; rather, I aim to make the process of buying & using your first car a smooth, enjoyable, and financially viable experience.

Excited to make the right choice? Stay with me as I show you how....

The purpose of writing this book is to educate first-time car buyers and help them in choosing the right car for them. I aim to empower all of you with the information needed to make an informed decision basis your needs & budget to make your first car & its usage a happy, prosperous, and memorable experience.

If you want to choose the right car for you, you mustn't make the seven cardinal mistakes that first-time car buyers in such cities often make. Here is a list of these common mistakes. In the following chapters, I will be talking about these in detail and showing you the right way of choosing & buying your car.

1. **Ignoring Research:** Not thoroughly researching different car models, their features, prices, and reviews can lead to making a decision that doesn't suit your needs or budget.

2. **Neglecting Budgeting:** Failing to establish a realistic budget can result in overspending or choosing a car with ongoing costs (such as maintenance, insurance, and fuel) that stretch your finances too thin.
3. **Skipping Test Drives:** Not test-driving multiple vehicles before making a decision can lead to dissatisfaction with the chosen car's comfort, handling, or performance.
4. **Underestimating Additional Costs:** Forgetting to factor in additional costs like insurance, registration fees, taxes, and accessories can cause budgetary strain later on.
5. **Ignoring Resale Value:** Overlooking the resale value of the chosen car model can result in financial losses when it's time to sell or upgrade in the future.
6. **Not Considering After-Sales Service:** Not researching the availability and quality of after-sales service, including authorized service centers and spare parts availability, can lead to inconvenience and higher maintenance costs down the line.
7. **Being Influenced by Emotions:** Making a decision based solely on emotions or external pressure without considering practical aspects like fuel efficiency, resale value, and maintenance costs can lead to regret later on.

Avoiding these mistakes requires patience, thorough research, and careful consideration of your needs, budget, and the specific conditions of the automotive market in two-tier cities in India.

Being aware of these mistakes and knowing what to do instead can serve as a structured guide for you, helping you navigate the complexities of purchasing your first car in two-tier cities in India while avoiding common pitfalls.

That is why this book is the most powerful tool for your decision-making when buying your first car. It is designed as a ready-reference guide to help you make the right choice step-by-step.

❍ ❍ ❍

Chapter 3

WHO AM I & WHY SHOULD YOU LISTEN TO ME?

Hello, my name is Gaurav Madhyani. I am an Automobile expert and specialist.

My tryst with automobiles began early on in my career as an automobile learner, 9 years back. Ever since then, it has never failed to impress me in terms of establishing lasting relationships with my clients and also in terms of providing them with world-class service.

I live and breathe the automobile industry daily, and making my customers happy continues to top my list every single day.

People don't just buy cars from us; they buy dreams instead!

They go through a lot of hard work to fulfil their dreams & desires, and I don't think there is any reason why they shouldn't be happy with their car.

And I have ample proof that I am succeeding in my mission of gifting people happiness & delight along with the cars they buy.

The Proof is in the Pudding/Facts

- That we have sold 11000+ cars in less than 9 years is a testimony to our service and guidance in helping you realize your dreams.
- Our bond isn't limited to selling; we believe in long-term relationships of joy & to this end, we have serviced more than 1.25 lakh vehicles in the same timeline. We have customers coming to us for service from even 300+ km away.
- We have a state-of-the-art facility & dedicated professionals providing great customer satisfaction, which is reflected in the many awards that we have received for customer satisfaction and the facility pan India.
- Based on our performance & customer delight, we received the LOI for the second Dealership within less than 2 years of the operation of the first showroom. How awesome is that!
- With more than 28000 satisfied families that trust us, it is no surprise that our Google rating is 4.9* and 4.7* as of 31st Jan 2024.

Chapter 4

TIP 1
THE ROADMAP TO RESEARCH

Embarking on the journey of purchasing your first car is an exhilarating experience, but it's crucial to start with a solid foundation of research. In this chapter, we'll explore the essential steps to take and the resources to utilize when researching your dream car.

Meet Riya

A recent college graduate living in a two-tier city in India, Riya has landed her first job and is eager to purchase her own car for commuting and weekend getaways with friends. Excited but unsure where to start, Riya dives into the world of car research.

Follow me as I show you how Riya should be choosing the car best suited to her....

Riya begins by consulting friends and family who own cars, seeking their advice on different makes and models. She learns about their experiences, preferences, and any regrets they may have had. Armed with this initial knowledge, Riya turns to the internet for more comprehensive research.

She explores automotive websites, forums, and social media groups dedicated to car enthusiasts. Riya reads reviews from experts and fellow drivers, paying attention to factors like fuel efficiency, safety features, and maintenance costs. She discovers that certain car models are better suited for city driving, while others excel on highways and rough terrain.

Here's a checklist of things that Riya needs to look for, research & understand, and educate herself on in context to her needs.

- Which segment vehicle should you choose? SUV/Sedan/ Hatchback
- Which brand should you go for? Popular brands that have workshops near your place or at least within 10-20 km of range.
- How to select variants and fuel for your car:
- Important: Safety tips to consider while buying a car.
- What accessories should you buy and why authorised dealers only? Never buy electrical accessories from outside as it impacts the warranty of your vehicle directly; it may lead to fire, and that can take away your money or even your life.
- The car type also depends on the person you are buying for: for example, if you are buying for a female/parents or teenage kids.
- Why understanding insurance in detail is important.
- RTO, Choice number, and Finance.
- How small things such as fuel lid side/tyre pressure/stepney etc. matter
- How to keep the vehicle parked for a long time if required.
- Advantages of the various features available in various brands/ models.
- An understanding of Traffic rules

Some of these checkpoints will be discussed in detail in this chapter, while others will be discussed in the following chapters.

The starting point of any car-buying journey should begin with understanding & deciding which segment of vehicle you should choose.

One size doesn't fit all; every person & family has different requirements and different choices.

Understanding Vehicle Segments

Primarily, cars are divided into three segments-

1. **SUVs**

   Technically, a sport utility vehicle (SUV) is a car classification that combines elements of road-going passenger cars with features from off-road vehicles, such as raised ground clearance and four-wheel drive. As per the GST council, an SUV should have an engine capacity exceeding 1,500cc, a length of more than 4,000 mm, and a ground clearance of 170 mm and above.

2. **Sedans**

   A sedan is a 4-door passenger car with a trunk that is separate from the passengers with a three-box body: the engine, the area for passengers, and the trunk. Throughout the generations, the definition of a sedan has been the same.

3. **Hatchbacks**

   A hatchback is a car with a rear door that swings upward to provide access to the main interior of the car as a cargo area rather than to a separate trunk.

   These segments are further subdivided as per the size and features:

   i. Entry level SUV

   ii. Subcompact SUV

   iii. Compact SUV

   iv. Full-size SUV

Even this can further be divided into 2WD/4WD or AWD, depending on the terrain you drive in, you can choose from this.

i. Compact Sedans

ii. Luxury sedans

iii. Ultra-luxury sedans

iv. Entry level hatch

v. Compact Hatch

v. Premium Hatch

vi. Crossovers

In India, the trend of SUVs is increasing rapidly; the highest-selling segments are Hatchbacks and SUVs only. While sedans hold their own place in the market, this segment is dying slowly, on the one hand, Sedans are more luxurious as compared to SUVs but SUVs are used for multiple purposes.

Now that you know the segments, study their feature and specifications & decide which works best for you.

The most important things to consider while buying your first car for both you and Riya are:

- Whether you travel solo or with family.
- Whether you carry substantial luggage or are light travellers with just backpacks.
- What are the road conditions near your house and place of work or any other areas that you frequently visit?
- Consider whether off-roading is done or not.
- Decide if you are looking for high seating or low seating.
- Who is going to drive primarily? Is it for a male/female/teenager/young adult?
- If older people will be using it, their challenges are different, they may have back issues. You should go for SUVs or Crossovers as

they won't be comfortable sitting too low.

- If the car is for long tours only, it should have a bigger boot space (bigger not in terms of litres but your luggage should fit properly).
- Colour plays an important role as dark colour absorbs heat and also look dirty after a couple of hours, so if you can't afford to wash your car daily or at least alternate days, go for the lighter shades.
- The colour of the interior is also very important; if the interior has too much white and you have kids, avoid such interiors.

> Riya travels light & the traffic around her home & office is chaotic, so she feels a Hatchback would be well suited for her; however, she also likes to travel to the mountains a lot and needs good road clearance, and a rugged car would be good for her. So as of now, Riya is open to looking at both Hatchbacks & SUVs but has definitely ruled out a Sedan as her first car.

Which Brand Should You Go For?

Almost all the brands available in our country produce excellent products. They have a team of experts who are paid just to ensure that every car comes equipped with comfort, reliability, and excellent fit and finish.

Don't let the power of advertising or celebrity endorsements influence your decision. Here are a few crucial things to consider before selecting the brand you want to go for.

- Check whether that brand offers a car within your budget.
- Check the distance of the nearest service centre of that brand from your place: it should ideally be not more than 30 km.

- Check what would be the resale value of the brand; after all, you will at some point change your car in future: maybe after 3-5 years down the line.
- Check carefully the reviews of the products you are comparing. Also, check the reviews of the dealers of that brand nearest to you.
- Don't forget to check the total number of cars sold by that particular brand every month. In the past, we have seen a few brands exit from India; this reduces the value of your car and may impact getting service in the future.
- A few important aspects to consider would be the choice of exterior and interior, and the performance of air conditioning, ride handling, power and pick-up etc.

Research Tips for Great Results

Start with Your Needs: Before diving into research, take some time to reflect on your lifestyle, daily commute, and future plans.

Consider factors such as the number of passengers you'll typically carry, the type of driving you'll be doing (city, highway, off-road), and any specific features or amenities that are non-negotiable for you.

Seek Advice: Don't hesitate to reach out to friends, family members, or colleagues who own cars. Their firsthand experiences can provide valuable insights and recommendations that you might not find elsewhere. Ask them about the pros and cons of their vehicles, any unexpected expenses or issues they've encountered, and whether they would recommend their car to others.

Utilize Online Resources: The internet is a treasure trove of information when it comes to researching cars. Explore automotive websites, forums, and social media groups dedicated to car enthusiasts. Read reviews from experts and fellow drivers, paying attention to both the positives and negatives of each car model. Look for information on factors such as fuel efficiency, reliability, safety ratings, and maintenance costs.

Think Long-Term: When researching car models, it's important to consider not just how they meet your current needs but also how they'll hold up over time. Look into factors such as the resale value of the vehicle, the availability of aftermarket parts and accessories, and the reputation of the manufacturer for reliability and customer service.

Choosing a car with strong long-term value can save you money and headaches down the road when it comes time to sell or trade-in your vehicle.

Look Beyond Brand Names: While it's natural to be drawn to well-known car brands, don't overlook lesser-known manufacturers that may offer better value for money or more suitable options for your needs.

Keep an open mind and consider a variety of makes and models before making your final decision. You might be surprised to find that a lesser-known brand offers the perfect combination of features, performance, and affordability for you.

By following these research tips and taking the time to explore your options thoroughly, like Riya, you can make an informed decision that sets you up for success with your first car.

Remember that purchasing a car is a significant investment, so it's worth putting in the effort upfront to ensure that you choose a vehicle that meets your needs, fits your budget, and brings you joy for years to come.

In the following chapters, I will share all the other pitfalls to avoid and the actions to take to ensure you choose the best first car for you.

Chapter 5

TIP 2 BUDGETING FOR YOUR JOURNEY

While understanding your needs and researching accordingly is crucial to buying the right car, money could be a roadblock on this journey.

In the pursuit of purchasing your first car, understanding and establishing a realistic budget is important. In this chapter, we'll delve into the crucial aspects of budgeting for your automotive project, ensuring that your financial foundation is strong and secure.

Riya's Budgeting Journey

So, you've already met Riya, a young professional living in a bustling two-tier city in India. Riya has been saving diligently for months, eager to fulfill her dream of owning a car. As she embarked on this exciting journey, she first analyzed her needs and researched what segments and brands suited her needs.

Riya also understands the importance of setting a practical budget to guide her decision-making process.

She begins by assessing her financial situation and taking stock of her income, savings, and monthly expenses. She calculates how much she can comfortably afford to allocate toward purchasing and maintaining a car without compromising her other financial goals and obligations.

With a clear understanding of her budgetary constraints, she researches various car models within her price range.

She considers not only the upfront cost of the vehicle but also the additional expenses associated with car ownership, such as insurance, fuel, servicing, and registration fees.

After careful consideration, she narrows down her options to a few affordable cars that meet her needs and preferences.

She compares the total cost of ownership for each model, factoring in both the initial purchase price and the long-term expenses, to ensure that she stays within her budget.

Earlier on in the previous chapter, based on her needs & preferences, Riya was toying between SUVs & Hatchbacks.

After a deep review and consideration of her finances, **ultimately, she selects a reliable and fuel-efficient hatchback that fits comfortably within her financial means, happy and confident** that she has made a sound decision that aligns with her budget and lifestyle.

Budgeting Tips for a Sound Investment

- **Evaluate Your Finances:** Begin by assessing your current financial situation, including your income, savings, and monthly expenses. Determine how much you can realistically afford to allocate toward purchasing and owning a car without straining your budget or jeopardizing your financial stability.

- **Consider All Costs:** When budgeting for your car purchase, don't just **focus on the upfront cost of the vehicle. Remember to factor in additional expenses such as insurance, fuel, servicing, maintenance, and registration fees.** Consider how these ongoing costs will impact your overall budget and adjust accordingly.
- **Set a Realistic Budget:** Establish a clear and realistic budget for your car purchase, taking into account both the total cost of the vehicle and the long-term expenses associated with ownership. Be honest with yourself about what you can afford, and resist the temptation to stretch your budget beyond its limits.
- **Don't be emotional about your decision** and go in for a car higher than your budget, even if it's a car with some memories or deep desires attached. Ultimately, the higher car budget will cause an ongoing strain on your finances, and you will not be able to enjoy it. Remember, this is just your first car; there will be plenty of time in life to fulfil those desires as well, once you consolidate your finances.
- **Also, do not stretch your budget merely to buy a car as a status symbol;** make sure to stay within your budget & buy value for money.
- **Shop Around for Financing:** If you plan to finance your car purchase, don't just settle for the first offer that you chance upon. Shop around for the best loan terms and interest rates. Compare offers from multiple lenders, including banks, credit unions, and online lenders, to ensure that you secure the most favorable financing option available to you.

Financing: An Overview

- Usually, 80% of the vehicles are financed in our country. One of the major reasons is that it is one of the cheapest loans in terms of interest rates and is one of the less complex finances (you can even close it after 6 months without any penalties).
- The interest rate on your loan will depend on your CIBIL (credit) score. It also depends on the rate at which RBI gives loans to the banks, and it fluctuates. Usually, people go in for a 5-year loan period. But there are options for up to 7 years also.
- To give you a ballpark indication, EMI per lakh for 5 years with a 9% interest rate comes to Rs 2075.82/- per month.
- So, if you are planning to take a loan of, say, Rs 8 lakh, the EMI would come to Rs 16,606.59/- per month
- There are a lot of EMI calculators available on apps and online that one can use to calculate the EMI.

Negotiate Wisely: When negotiating the purchase price of your car, **be prepared to haggle and negotiate with the dealer.** Research the fair market value of the vehicle beforehand and use this information to leverage a better deal. Don't be afraid to walk away if the dealer isn't willing to meet your budgetary requirements.

Plan for Future Expenses: Anticipate future expenses such as repairs, upgrades, and potential emergencies, and set aside funds in your budget to cover these costs. Building a financial cushion will provide peace of mind and help you avoid financial strain down the road.

Be Flexible: While it's essential to stick to your budget, be open to adjusting your expectations or considering alternative options if necessary.

Keep an eye out for sales, promotions, or pre-owned vehicles that may offer better value for money without compromising on quality or reliability.

By following these budgeting tips and maintaining a disciplined approach to your finances, like Riya, you can ensure that your first car purchase is a financially responsible decision that sets you up for success in the long run. Remember that establishing a realistic budget is the first step towards achieving your aspirations while maintaining financial stability and peace of mind.

Chapter 6

TIP 3
TEST DRIVE ESSENTIALS

Test driving is a critical step in the car-buying process, allowing you to experience firsthand how a vehicle performs on the road and whether it meets your expectations.

In this chapter, we'll explore the importance of test drives and provide essential tips for making the most of this opportunity.

Believe What You See & Drive

By now, you all know Riya very well; you know how wisely and meticulously she makes all her decisions, researching, budgeting, and comparing in detail.

Now that she has compared everything online and has narrowed down her options to a few contenders, Riya takes the crucial step of visiting dealerships to see the vehicles in person. She examines the interiors, checks the legroom and cargo space, and asks the sales representatives detailed questions about each car's specifications and features.

After shortlisting potential cars, excited but cautious, she decides to schedule test drives to get a feel for each vehicle before making her final decision.

She begins her test-driving journey by visiting local dealerships and expressing her interest in specific car models. The sales representatives are friendly and accommodating, allowing her to explore the interiors, examine the features, and ask questions about each vehicle's specifications and performance.

As she takes each car out for a spin, **she pays close attention to how it performs on different types of roads, from crowded city streets to open highways. She evaluates factors such as acceleration, braking, steering responsiveness, and overall comfort, noting any differences between the various models she's testing.**

During the test drives, Riya also takes the opportunity to test out the car's features and amenities, such as the infotainment system, climate control, and driver-assistance technologies. **She assesses the ease of use, functionality, and convenience of these features, considering how they enhance her driving experience.**

After completing all her test drives, she reflects on her experiences and carefully weighs the pros and cons of each car. Armed with valuable insights from her test-driving adventures, she ultimately selects the perfect vehicle that meets her needs, fits her budget, and brings her joy every time she gets behind the wheel.

Test Driving Tips to Make the Right Choice

- **Schedule Multiple Test Drives:** Don't settle for the first car you test drive. Schedule appointments to test drive multiple vehicles within your price range and compare their performance, features, and overall feel on the road. Testing different models will give you a better understanding of what you like and don't like in a car.

Take test drives and compare all the cars on the same day, if possible.

- **Plan Your Test Drive Route:** Choose a test drive route that includes a variety of road conditions, such as city streets, highways, and winding roads. This will allow you to assess how the car performs in different environments and simulate the type of driving you'll be doing daily.
- **Bring Along a Checklist:** Create a checklist of features and qualities you're looking for in a car, such as fuel efficiency, safety features, comfort, and storage space. Use this checklist during your test drives to evaluate each vehicle systematically and ensure that it meets your criteria.
- **Pay Attention to Comfort and Ergonomics:** Spend some time adjusting the driver's seat, steering wheel, and mirrors to find a comfortable driving position. Pay attention to factors such as visibility, seating comfort, and ergonomics to ensure that you'll be comfortable during long drives. Headroom is also very important, especially for tall people; make sure that you can get in and out of the vehicle comfortably without hitting your head in the car.
- **Test Out Key Features:** Take the time to test out the car's key features and amenities, such as the infotainment system, air conditioning, and driver-assistance technologies. Make sure that these features are easy to use, intuitive, and enhance your overall driving experience.
- **Listen for Unusual Noises:** Pay attention to any unusual noises or vibrations during the test drive, as these could be indicators of underlying mechanical issues. Listen for engine noise, rattles, squeaks, or clunks, and bring them to the attention of the sales representative for further inspection.
- **Trust Your Instincts:** Ultimately, trust your instincts and gut feeling about each car you test drive. If something doesn't feel

right or if you have reservations about a particular vehicle, don't ignore them. Take the time to explore other options until you find the perfect car that meets all your requirements and feels right for you.

By following these test drive tips and taking the time to thoroughly evaluate each vehicle, like Riya, you can make an informed decision that ensures you'll enjoy many miles of happy driving in your new car. Remember that test driving is your opportunity to experience the car firsthand and ensure that it meets your expectations in terms of performance, comfort, and overall satisfaction.

Chapter 7

Tip 4
Beyond the Sticker Price: Decoding Hidden Costs

Purchasing a car involves more than just the upfront cost of the vehicle. Buying a physical car is merely the first step. There are further costs involved in the buying process that first-time car buyers sometimes are not aware of, and they come as a shock to them.

In this chapter, we'll explore the various hidden costs associated with car ownership and provide essential tips for budgeting and planning to ensure you're financially prepared for the road ahead.

Believe What You See & Drive

So, in the last chapter, following Riya's journey to choose her first car, we know that Riya visited various dealerships in person.

As she explored different car models and visited dealerships, **she quickly realized that there's more to consider than just the sticker price.**

She learned about the various hidden costs associated with car ownership, including insurance, fuel, servicing, maintenance, and registration fees.

So, she took time to research and estimate these additional expenses, carefully factoring them into the budgeting calculations that she had worked on earlier. **Doing this exercise, she understood that failing to account for these hidden costs could lead to financial strain down the road and impact her overall financial stability.**

With a clear understanding of the total cost of ownership for each car she was considering, she was able to make an informed decision that aligned with her budget and lifestyle. **As a result, she selected a fuel-efficient and low-maintenance vehicle that met her needs while minimizing ongoing expenses.**

Now, Riya's mind is at peace, and she feels confident, knowing that she's made a financially responsible decision that has set her up for success in the long run.

Tips to Factor in Hidden Costs

- **Consider Registration and Taxes:** Don't forget to factor in registration fees, road tax, and any other government-mandated expenses associated with purchasing and owning a car. These costs can vary depending on your location and the type of vehicle you're purchasing, so be sure to research and budget for them accordingly.

  The RTO department falls under the State Government; therefore, the price varies from state to state.

  As per the rule, a dealer cannot deliver a vehicle without a number plate to the customer.

  The payment for getting a number of your choice varies from state to state. Once you have paid for the choice number, it is valid for the next 90 days, and you can use that number for any vehicle you buy in that period.

Also, remember that the colour of the number plate indicates the type of vehicle it is, so use the right colour:

1. **White:** For common-use private vehicles
2. **Yellow:** For commercial use
3. **Green:** For electric vehicles

- **Budget for Accessories and Upgrades:** Consider any additional accessories or upgrades you may want to add to your car, such as a navigation system, upgraded sound system, or protective coatings. These optional extras can add to the overall cost of the vehicle, so be sure to budget for them accordingly if they're important to you.
- **Estimate Fuel Expenses:** Consider the fuel efficiency of the car you're interested in and estimate your monthly fuel expenses based on your typical driving habits. Keep in mind that fuel prices can fluctuate, so it's essential to build some flexibility into your budget to accommodate potential changes in fuel costs.
- **Budget for Servicing and Maintenance:** Cars require regular servicing and maintenance to keep them running smoothly and prevent costly repairs down the road. Research the servicing schedules and maintenance costs for the vehicles you're considering and budget accordingly. It's also a good idea to set aside funds for unexpected repairs or emergencies to avoid financial strain in the event of a breakdown or mechanical issue.
- **Factor in Insurance Costs:** Before purchasing a car, obtain insurance quotes for the vehicles you're considering. Insurance premiums can vary significantly depending on factors such as the make and model of the car and from where you are buying. Factor these costs into your budgeting calculations to ensure that you can afford the insurance premiums for your chosen vehicle.

Understanding Insurance in Detail

With online apps today, it has become very easy to compare and get insurance, but the real challenge comes after a mishap. Many times, these apps reduce the IDV (Insurance Declared Value) to reduce the premium, while you don't understand this, this increases the chance of total loss in case of a major accident and you get less amount in your bank in these cases. So, check carefully as to what the IDV is, and do not be lured by lower premiums.

Also, there are many types of add-ons in insurance that you must consider and choose as per need and budget, such as

1. **Engine protection:** It helps cover the external damage to the engine during any accident. One of my teachers saved Rs 60,000/- because of this in 2017, the engine work was covered in the insurance after her car met with an accident. It is a useful add-on to have.
2. **Return to Invoice:** Generally, when we talk about car insurance, it is equal to 95% of the ex-showroom price, but this type of insurance, though a little bit costlier, covers 100% amount of the ex-showroom as well as the amount of RTO and Insurance as well.

There are many other small add-ons available, but most people ignore them due to price comparison. No one wants to meet with an accident, but life happens, and if we have the right insurance, we can at least reduce our worries after that. So, look at all add-on insurances carefully and consider buying them if you can.

Most insurance companies provide add-on insurance 2 times in a year, and after that, the policy is treated as a normal policy. But there are a few insurance companies from special brokers which provide unlimited addon cover and they provide the service for any number of times. So, research and choose carefully.

NOTE: No insurance company gives more than 2 add-on insurance for commercial vehicles/taxis.

Super Tip: Go for the unlimited times add-on, and whenever any scratch or minor accident occurs, you can go for the claim.

Knowing that insurance will be an additional cost and understanding how to choose insurance is great, however, it is even better to know how to claim insurance correctly by understanding the conditions that lead to the rejection of claims.

1. If the person driving at the time of the accident does not have a valid licence/the claim will be rejected. Therefore, ensure that you or anyone else driving has a valid driving license.
2. If you do not file an FIR in case of major accidents, the claim gets rejected, as 3rd party damage is also the responsibility of insurance companies, and they want to make sure what happened at the time of the accident from the FIR.
3. If the person driving is a learner and is not under the supervision of a permanent valid license holder, the claim will be rejected.
4. If the claim is not initiated within 10-15 days of the accident, it will be rejected; ensure that you claim in time.

Of course, there are a few more cases where claims get rejected, but these are the most common scenarios, and as a first-time car owner, you must be aware of them and comply with them.

- **Plan for Depreciation:** Keep in mind that cars depreciate in value over time, which can impact their long-term resale value. While depreciation isn't a direct expense, it's important to consider how it will affect your overall financial picture and factor it into your budgeting calculations when purchasing a car.

- **Build a Financial Cushion:** Finally, it's essential to build a financial cushion to cover unexpected expenses or emergencies that may arise during your ownership of the vehicle. Set aside funds in a separate savings account specifically earmarked for car-related expenses to ensure that you're prepared for any unforeseen costs that may arise.

By considering these hidden costs and budgeting accordingly, like (Arjun and Nisha)? You can ensure that you're financially prepared for the responsibilities of car ownership and avoid any financial surprises along the way.

Remember that being proactive and thorough in your budgeting and planning will set you up for success and allow you to enjoy your new car with confidence and peace of mind like Riya.

Chapter 8

TIP 5
MAXIMIZING VALUE: THE RESALE FACTOR

When purchasing a car, it's essential to consider not only its initial cost but also its long-term value. In this chapter, we'll explore the importance of resale value and provide essential tips for choosing a car that holds its value well over time and is not a disappointment when it's time for an upgrade.

Riya Follows a Great Example!

Meet Sameer, Riya's senior in college and a good friend and mentor. Riya had witnessed Sameer's car-buying journey nearly 5 years ago. He had been super excited to purchase his first car and had researched different models to find the perfect fit. Delving deeper into his research, Riya had seen Sameer learn about the importance of considering resale value when making his decision.

He had understood that a car was a significant investment, and he had decided to choose a vehicle that would hold its value well over time. He knew that selecting a car with a strong resale value would not only save him money in the long run but also make it easier to upgrade to a new vehicle in the future.

Armed with this knowledge, he had carefully evaluated the resale value of the cars he was considering. He had looked into factors such as brand reputation, reliability, popularity, and depreciation rates to gauge each vehicle's long-term value proposition.

After thorough research and consideration, Sameer selected a car with a reputation for holding its value well and minimal depreciation over time.

Even today, Riya can recall how confident he had been in his decision, knowing that he'd chosen a vehicle that not only met his current needs but also offered strong long-term value.

And now, years later, just as Riya is buying her first car, Sameer has decided to upgrade to a new car. he & Riya are pleasantly surprised to discover that his current vehicle has retained much of its resale value.

Thanks to his careful consideration of resale value when making his initial purchase, Sameer can today sell his car for a competitive price and put the proceeds towards his new vehicle.

Riya is not only happy for him, but she is determined to follow his example and research thoroughly to ensure she chooses a car with a great resale value.

The Goodbye Gift:
Tips for Maximizing Resale Value

- **Choose a Popular Model:** Opt for a car that is popular and in high demand in the market. Popular models tend to hold their value better over time, as there is a consistently strong demand for them in the resale market.

- **Consider Brand Reputation:** Research the reputation of the car manufacturer and choose a brand known for producing reliable, high-quality vehicles. Cars from reputable brands tend to have better resale value due to their perceived reliability and durability.
- **Evaluate Depreciation Rates:** Look into the depreciation rates of the cars you're considering and **choose a model with minimal depreciation over time.** Cars that retain their value well are more likely to fetch a higher resale price when it comes time to sell or trade-in.
- **Opt for Timeless Designs:** Select a car with a timeless design and classic styling that won't go out of fashion quickly. **Avoid trendy or niche models that may have limited appeal in the resale market.**

  Common colours like white or silver will give better resale value in the future as these colours are a choice of many.
- **Maintain Your Car Regularly:** Keep up with regular maintenance and servicing to ensure that your car remains in good condition and retains its value over time. A well-maintained vehicle is more attractive to potential buyers and commands a higher resale price.
- **Keep Mileage in Check:** Be mindful of your car's mileage and try to keep it as low as possible. Lower-mileage vehicles typically command higher resale prices, as they are perceived to have less wear and tear and potentially more life left in them.
- **Document Service History:** Keep thorough records of your car's service history, including receipts, invoices, and maintenance records. **A documented service history demonstrates to potential buyers that the car has been well cared for** and can help justify a higher resale price. Although one can find the history of any car from the dealership, many don't want to do the tedious exercise.

- **Invest in Protective Measures:** Consider investing in protective measures such as paint protection film, rust-proofing, and interior treatments to keep your car looking its best and protect its resale value.

By considering these tips and prioritizing resale value when making your car purchase, like Sameer & Riya, you can ensure that you're making a sound investment that will pay off in the long run.

Remember that choosing a car with a strong resale value not only saves you money over time but also makes it easier to upgrade to a new vehicle when the time comes.

Your first car will end up giving you a gift even when you are saying goodbye to it.

Chapter 9

TIP 6
SERVICE STATIONS AND SPARE PARTS: NAVIGATING AFTER-SALES

After-sales service is a crucial aspect of car ownership, ensuring that your vehicle remains in top condition and performs optimally over time. In this chapter, we'll explore the importance of after-sales service and provide essential tips for navigating service stations and spare parts in two-tier cities in India.

Maintenance Maximizes Performance & Value

Riya had seen first-hand what great resale value her friend Sameer's car had given. **She also knew that one big reason for it was the great condition the car was in. Sameer had been well aware of the importance of after-sales service in maintaining his vehicle's performance, reliability, and, thus, resale value.**

Riya remembered how Sameer had researched local service stations and authorized service centers in their city. He had sought recommendations from friends, family, and online reviews to identify reputable service providers with a track record of excellence in customer service and technical expertise.

Once he had selected a service center, he scheduled his first maintenance appointment and took his car in for servicing. All his research and diligence had paid off- he was impressed by the professionalism and efficiency of the service staff, who performed a thorough inspection of his vehicle and addressed any issues or concerns promptly.

As Sameer continued to drive his car and accumulate miles, **he made it a point to adhere to the recommended servicing schedule and bring his vehicle in for regular maintenance.** He understands that routine servicing is essential for prolonging the lifespan of his car and preventing costly repairs down the road.

In addition to servicing, he had also familiarized himself with the availability of spare parts for his car model. He learned about the importance of using genuine OEM (Original Equipment Manufacturer) parts to maintain the integrity and performance of his vehicle and made sure to purchase spare parts from authorized dealerships or reputable suppliers.

Thanks to his proactive approach to after-sales service, his car remained in excellent condition, delivering reliable performance and peace of mind on every journey until he upgraded just a month ago. And it had given him great resale value, too.

Now that Riya was getting her first car, she was determined to follow his lead and maintain it regularly on time to keep it in peak performance.

Tips for Navigating After-Sales

- **Research Local Service Stations:** Take the time to research local service stations and authorized service centers in your area. Seek recommendations from friends, family, and online reviews to identify reputable service providers with a proven track record of excellence in customer service and technical expertise.

- **Adhere to Maintenance Schedule:** Follow the manufacturer's recommended servicing schedule and bring your car in for regular maintenance at the specified intervals. Routine servicing is essential for keeping your vehicle in top condition and preventing costly repairs down the road.
- **Use Genuine OEM Parts:** When replacing parts or components in your car, always opt for genuine OEM (Original Equipment Manufacturer) parts. Genuine parts are designed specifically for your car model and are guaranteed to fit and perform as intended, ensuring the longevity and reliability of your vehicle.

OEMs: Your Ace Card!

Nowadays, all OEMs are working hard to provide buyers with different options for accessories and spare parts. Not only do these accessories fit the best but also come with a certain period of warranty.

Getting fitment from outside vendors means removing the cherry from the top and compromising with low-quality material for the same cost many times.

If you are looking for electrical component fitments, ensure that you only trust OEMs, as it will directly impact the following:

1. **Warranty:** Your warranty lapses when anyone from the outside cuts or twists the original setting of the wire.
2. **Insurance:** The insurance company will delve into and find out the details of where you got your fitments done and will not give a single Rupee in a claim in case of any incidence.
3. **Life:** It has been observed that many vehicles catch fire while running over the roads. In most cases, the fire starts with a short circuit from an electrical wire. Ensure you only use original, quality wire.

- **Verify Technician Qualifications:** Before entrusting your car to a service center, verify the qualifications and expertise of the service technicians. Ensure that they are certified and trained to work on your specific car model and that they use the latest diagnostic tools and equipment for servicing and repairs.
- **Understand Warranty Coverage:** Familiarize yourself with the warranty coverage provided by the manufacturer for your car. Understand what is covered under the warranty and for how long, as well as any conditions or limitations that may apply. This will help you make informed decisions about servicing and repairs and avoid unnecessary expenses.
- **Budget for Maintenance Costs:** Factor in maintenance costs when budgeting for car ownership and set aside funds for routine servicing, repairs, and spare parts. Having a financial cushion dedicated to car maintenance will ensure that you're prepared for any unexpected expenses that may arise.
- **Stay Proactive:** Be proactive about maintaining your car and addressing any issues or concerns promptly. Pay attention to warning signs, such as strange noises, dashboard warning lights, or changes in performance, and address them promptly to prevent further damage or issues.

By following these after-sales service tips and taking a proactive approach to maintaining your vehicle, like Sameer and Riya, you can ensure that your car remains in top condition and delivers reliable performance for years to come.

Remember that after-sales service is an essential aspect of car ownership, and investing time and effort into finding reputable service providers and maintaining your vehicle properly will pay off in the long run.

Chapter 10

TIP 7
STEERING CLEAR OF EMOTIONAL PITFALLS

When purchasing your first car, it's easy to get swept up in emotions and impulses. However, making decisions based solely on emotions can lead to regrets and financial strain down the road.

While this advice may sound very simple on the face of it, it can lead to lots of stress, anxiety & disappointment later on.

In this chapter, we'll explore the importance of staying rational and practical during the car-buying process and provide essential tips for avoiding emotional pitfalls.

Naina's Emotional Disaster

Let's meet Naina, another friend of Riya's. She too recently bought a Car.

Naina has been dreaming of owning a car since she got her driver's license, and she's excited to finally make her dream a reality. Eager to find the perfect car, she starts her search with enthusiasm and optimism.

As she visits dealerships and test drives various car models, she finds herself drawn to a sleek and stylish sports car that catches her eye. Despite its high price tag and impracticality for her daily commute, she can't help but feel a strong emotional attachment to the car.

Ignoring rational considerations like fuel efficiency, maintenance costs, and resale value, she decides to splurge on the sports car, believing that it will bring her happiness and fulfillment.

However, as time goes on, she begins to regret her impulsive decision as **she struggles to afford the ongoing expenses associated with owning the car.**

Frustrated and overwhelmed by the financial strain, **Naina is in a really bad situation and is now defaulting on her EMIs. Also, the car is not at all fuel-efficient, and to add to her woes, fuel costs keep rising. So frustrating is the situation that Naina barely takes the car out due to the high cost of fuel.**

Today, she realizes the importance of staying rational and practical during the car-buying process. She wishes she had taken the time to consider her needs, budget, and long-term goals more carefully before making such a significant decision.

Finally, God has heard her prayers; a relative is willing to buy her car at a decent price and is ready to pay upfront so that she can first pay off her loan and then transfer the car to his name. Naina is relieved to get the car off her hands.

Determined to learn from her mistakes, she vows to approach future car purchases with a more rational and practical mindset.

She understands that while emotions are natural, they shouldn't override rational considerations when it comes to making important financial decisions like buying a car.

Having witnessed Naina's emotional debacle, Riya is determined not to let emotions get in the way of buying the right car..

Tips for Avoiding Emotional Pitfalls

- **Define Your Needs:** Before you start shopping for a car, take some time to define your needs and priorities. Consider factors such as your daily commute, lifestyle, budget, and long-term goals to determine what features and qualities are most important to you in a car.
- **Set a Budget and Stick to It:** Establish a realistic budget for your car purchase and stick to it. Avoid the temptation to overspend or stretch your budget beyond its limits, as this can lead to financial strain and regret down the road.
- **Do Your Research:** Thoroughly research different car models, their features, prices, and reviews before making a decision. Consider factors such as fuel efficiency, maintenance costs, resale value, and reliability to ensure that you choose a car that meets your needs and fits your budget.
- **Take Your Time:** Don't rush into a decision. Take your time to explore your options, schedule test drives, and compare different vehicles before making a final choice. Avoid making impulsive decisions based on emotions or external pressure.
- **Consult Others:** Seek advice from friends, family members, or trusted experts who have experience buying cars. Their insights and perspectives can help you make a more informed decision and avoid common pitfalls.
- **Consider the Long-Term:** Think about the long-term implications of your car purchase, including ongoing expenses like insurance, fuel, maintenance, and resale value. Choose a car that aligns with your long-term goals and financial priorities rather than just satisfying your short-term desires.
- **Listen to Your Gut:** While it's essential to stay rational and practical, don't ignore your intuition and gut feelings about a

particular car or decision. If something doesn't feel right, take a step back and reassess before moving forward.

- **Seek Professional Advice:** If you're unsure about a particular aspect of the car-buying process, don't hesitate to seek professional advice from a trusted financial advisor or car expert. They can provide valuable guidance and help you make a more informed decision.

  Most importantly, remember that a car is a tool, a means of transportation that needs to be functional, practical, and comfortable, but is very certainly not a status symbol, a fashion ite,m or an emotional anchor- especially if it's your first car.

By following these tips and staying rational and practical during the car-buying process, like Naina & Riya, you can avoid emotional pitfalls and make a decision that you'll feel confident and satisfied with in the long run.

Remember that while emotions are natural, they shouldn't override rational considerations when it comes to making important financial decisions like purchasing a car.

Chapter 11

BONUS TIPS BECAUSE WE ALL LOVE SURPRISES

How do you select a variant for your car?

- The difference between the variants of any particular car is that of the features it has. Depending on the number of features, the price goes up.
- **Sometimes, the difference between the lowest variant and the top one can vary up to 60%.**
- This is because the OEMs know the aspirations of the Indian market.
- Since variants are all about features, let's discuss some prominent features and their advantages.
- **Power Windows:** 2-door power windows are a standard today, and soon we will see all cars coming with 4-door power windows, which help in operating the windows from the driver's seat
- **Push start button:** Push start button means that the car comes with a keyless entry also, which means that you can unlock the car by pressing the black button on the handle of the car, it gives a premium feel and is easier to operate.

- **Rear A/C vent:** A few OEMs make sure that their cars cool the entire cabin as soon as possible, so they provide the rear A/C vents for the rear passengers, which helps cool the car fast. This is a useful feature to have.
- **Alloy wheels:** They look sportier and help in better grip as they cut the air properly.
- **Sunroof:** Sunroofs help in cooling the car faster (as hot air rises up) and also allow nature into the car while offering you great views. There are different sizes of Sunroofs and people like to have a panoramic sunroof. At night, when the blinds are open and the person can see the moon and street light from inside, one feels close to nature.
- **High-end speakers:** Many OEMs provide world-class speakers to give the best audio experience.
- **Wireless charging:** Wireless charging ports are common these days. This is an essential feature to have in today's times, where our phones are our lifelines. This feature helps in charging the phone while on the move.
- **Rear window blinds:** The Sun shines bright in most of the cities in India; this feature helps in shading the rear seats, thus making the ride comfortable.
- **Rear parking camera along with sensors:** This helps in parking your car smoothly without the help of anyone or without needing to worry about what is behind.
- **ADAS:** ADAS is one of the new features that is now coming with almost every high-end car and also with many cars under Rs 15 lakhs. ADAS means Advance Driving Assistance System. Put in simple words, it will alarm the driver before a collision or will apply the brake by itself and can also self-drive the car without any human intervention. It has two functions: to detect and to act.

- Currently, level 1 and level 2 ADAS are common. In level 1, the car sends a signal to the driver to brake the car, and in level 2, it brakes itself when some object comes in front (auto brakes). This system will save a lot of accidents in the future and is one of the most important safety features.
- **Air purifiers:** Pollution is increasing, and you cannot deny it. These air purifiers may not control the air quality by 100%, but they work better (at least 60% when the filters are cleaned from time to time), which is a blessing in disguise. With the AQI mostly at alarming levels, this is a great feature to have.

A Few Useful Accessories one can buy

- **Door Visors:** It is mainly used to open the windows a little but without allowing rainwater to come inside. Very useful to prevent fog during rains.
- **Dustbins:** OEMs are very concerned about little details, and this is one of the examples. With a dustbin inside, you can keep the trash generated during drives, small packets, etc., in these without littering your car or the roads to dispose it later when you get home.
- **Air inflators:** These are inflators that you can use when your tyres lose pressure
- **Chrome Garnish:** Many teenagers prefer to get attention and want the car to look out of the crowd, and these accessories highlight the headlamps, tail lamps, boot, and other curves of your car.
- **Seat Covers:** This is very useful if you have kids or if you eat inside your vehicle. One suggestion: use the original seats provided by OEM for the first few months and later go for seat covers. Don't forget to use the right seat cover as the cars with 6 airbags have airbags attached to the seat only, so a special seat cover is designed for them. The wrong seat cover can disallow seat covers to inflate and can be fatal.

Now, the key thing to remember and apply here is this:

Never go for the features that you will never use; always look for the features that are important for you and your family.

Kids love sunroofs, teenagers want an online tracking system and a great audio experience, people who work in different cities want their parents to have cars with tracking devices so that they can be sure where their parents are and so on, choose wisely.

Also, some features will only be available from OEMs; however, nowadays, almost 80% of the features are available in the form of accessories in the local market, but the feel and finish cannot be compared to the original ones (company-fitted). It is, therefore, advised to get all features and accessories from OEMs for a better experience and to get great value for money.

Selecting a Fuel Type for Your Car

This will depend on the type of usage and commuting you have and on the local state government rules; for example, Diesel is banned in a few cities.

- If your usage is less than 1000 km/month, you should prefer petrol.
- If you run your car more than 2000 km/month, you can prefer diesel or CNG.
- If your daily commute is roughly 100 km and the infrastructure in your area of usage is good, an electric vehicle is recommended; it is very affordable, efficient, and environment-friendly.
- **Right now, India's infrastructure is growing rapidly; with time, we will see fast chargers installed every few km, but currently, if you are planning to buy electric vehicles, make sure that the charger is installed at your home and office as well.**

- Fuel Cell or Hydrogen is also one of the upcoming fuel options; shortly, it will solve the problem of time consumed in charging electrical vehicles.
- Talking about pollution, diesel is the most polluting fuel, but it gives good mileage.
- Hybrid technology is one of the highly accepted and useful technologies, but it is costlier as compared to diesel and much costlier as compared to petrol engines.
- CNG is also a very good option, and nowadays, people get a lot of options for OEM-fitted CNG kits. They also produce less pollution as compared to diesel engines.
- Electrical vehicles produce the least pollution, but in a broader perspective, it depends on the way the electricity is produced (in India, we are shifting towards cleaner sources of electricity like solar, but still today a huge part of electricity is produced from coal).

Safety tips to consider while buying a car

Simply put, a car is a metal box that carries us from one place to another. On **average, 18 people die in accidents every hour in India (as per the Ministry of Transport 2022 report). Shocking, right???**

So, **it becomes very important to go for a safer car. How can one know if the car is safe or not?**

There are bodies that do BCAP and NCAP rating. These ratings tell us how safe a car is, these data are available online, and they give a rating out of 5 for the safety of the vehicle. They practically test the car under articulated conditions and see what impact happens after the accident to the passengers sitting inside the car.

Few OEMs have started 6 airbags as standard, and slowly, the transport department is also working towards getting better and safer cars for Indian roads.

In past there have been instances where the car that was in India was having a poor NCAP rating and the same car in Europe was designed with better safety as the requirements vary from country to country.

India has come up with a new NCAP rating known as Bharat NCAP, currently, it is not mandatory for OEMs, and any car that OEM is willing to send for a test is welcomed, and the test will be performe,d and the results will be shared publicly.

As mentioned in the features section earlier, ADAS is one of the new features that is now coming with almost every high-end car and also with many cars under Rs 15 lakhs. ADAS means Advance Driving Assistance System; in simple words,s it will alarm the driver before a collision.

Currently, level 1 and level 2 ADAS are common. In level 1, the car sends a signal to the driver to brake the car, and in level 2, it breaks itself when some object comes in front (auto brakes). This system will save a lot of accidents in the future and is one of the most important safety features.

Some Safety DON'Ts

- Coming to sunroofs: Though they seem beautiful and are a symbol of luxury today, they are equally dangerous, they reduce the overall strength of the car and also it is very dangerous if someone is standing out from the sunroof and the vehicle is braked suddenly or meets with an accident, the person standing out from the sunroof will tend to move out because of the inertia.
- Accessories like guards are banned in India but many people still go for them to save their car from damage, however, this can be

dangerous, due to this guard, the airbags are unable to open and the people inside might get badly hurt in case of accidents (don't be more concerned about the car than your lives)

Tips for your vehicle's long life

The vehicle should be serviced at an authorized service center only; if not, the warranty will be affected.

- **Change the stepney only for certain KMs:** the stepney remains new until used, many times stepney is used after 20,000 km also, many OEMs give a stepney that is 1 inch lower in size, this is because it is to be used for emergency only. If one tyre has a better grip and the other 3 do not have that type of grip, there are chances of drifting.
- Don't ignore any unusual or squeaky sounds; get them checked out ASAP. They could mean bigger problems.
- You might be attracted to stickers that are available in the market to look different, but they damage the original paint of the vehicle.
- Wash your car frequently but carefully.
- Clean your car interiors as well, as these collect dust & dirt too.
- Park your car in a safe area to protect it from dust, leaves, branches, debris, etc.
- **Body cover:** It's better to cover your car with a body cover if you are going out or won't be using it for 10-15 days; it helps increase the overall life of the vehicle.
- Don't overload your car either with luggage in the trunk/on the roof or with passengers. This can reduce its lifespan.
- **Fuel lid:** there is a fuel logo (pump) with an arrow in it, this indicates the side in which the lid is present. (So that one can navigate the vehicle at the petrol pump accordingly without getting confused as to which side to park.

Some fun yet vital tips

Change in name: Usually, as per our tradition, the surnames of girls change after marriage; it is important to note here that getting the name corrected in such cases is very critical. In case of an accident, the insurance company sees that the name in RTO and Insurance should be the same, also they will require documents with the same name for address verification and sign verification, and in case one is not able to provide the same, the insurance company is not liable to cover the incident.

In case one is buying a used car, it is the responsibility of the new owner to get the name change in the insurance as well after the name is changed in RTO because of the above reason only.

Chapter 12

DRIVING OFF JOYFULLY........

In conclusion, purchasing your first car is a significant milestone filled with excitement, anticipation, and a sense of accomplishment.

I have simulated that journey for you in the pages of this book.

Throughout this journey, we've together explored the essential steps to take and the common pitfalls to avoid to ensure that your car-buying experience is smooth, satisfying, and financially responsible.

From laying the groundwork with thorough research to navigating after-sales service and staying rational in the face of emotional impulses, **we've covered all the bases to help you make an informed decision that meets your needs, fits your budget, and brings you joy for years to come.**

We've learned the importance of defining your needs, setting a realistic budget, and considering long-term factors like maintenance costs and resale value. We've explored the significance of test drives in evaluating a car's performance and features and the importance of after-sales service in maintaining your vehicle's reliability and longevity.

Through real-life stories (names changed) of Riya, Sameer & Naina, we've seen first-hand the impact of careful planning and informed decision-making on the car-buying process.

Whether it's avoiding common mistakes, maximizing value, or steering clear of emotional pitfalls, in each chapter, I've provided valuable insights and practical tips to guide you on your journey to car ownership.

As you set out on the exciting adventure of actually buying your first car, remember to stay proactive, diligent, and open-minded. **Seek advice from trusted sources, take your time to explore your options, and trust your instincts when making decisions**.

Following the guidance provided in this guide, you can navigate the car-buying process with confidence and ease, ensuring that your first car purchase is a rewarding and fulfilling experience.

Ultimately, purchasing your first car is more than just acquiring a mode of transportation—it's a symbol of independence, freedom, and new beginnings.

With the knowledge and tools gained from this guide, you're ready to make a decision that reflects your personal needs, preferences, and aspirations, setting you on the road to countless adventures and memories ahead.

As it comes to the end of this book, please know that this is not the end of our journey together. Due to page constraints, I can't write all the tips & info needed to make your best choice.

Here, I have given you the first 7 points; believe me, I have 7 more.

For those of you who want to ensure that your first car-buying journey is a completely seamless and fool-proof process, I invite you to book a 1-2-1 appointment at the Calendly link below so that we can discuss this in detail and develop a buying plan tailored to get the right car for you.

https://calendly.com/gauravmadhyani

Because this industry has given me so much, I consider it my duty to serve my community.

www.ingramcontent.com/pod-product-compliance
Lightning Source LLC
Chambersburg PA
CBHW072244240926
51846CB00012B/603
* 9 7 8 9 3 6 3 3 8 1 2 5 4 *